PEELING, DEALING, AND HEALING

G. Allen

Copyright © 2016 G. Allen

All rights reserved.

ISBN: 0998394521
ISBN-13: 978-0998394527

CONTENTS

FOREWORD v
Adrift 7
Cleaning House 8
Reality 9
Driftwood 10
Regrets 11
Jagged Seams 12
On the Trying Side 13
Boundaries 14
Shadows in the Corner 15
Swing Shift 16
On the Edge 17
What Goes 'Round 18
She 19
Thorns 20
Envy 21
Pulling a Double 22
Perennial Passion 23
The Land of Know 24
Mountain Tale 25
Options 26

Leaf	27
Intimate Castles	28
Life on the Ledge	29
Piece of Peace	30
Spring Cleaning	33
Words of Wisdom	34
Birth, Rebirth	35
Opening the Door	36
Sadness	37
Growth	38
For Just a Moment	39
Hammock Time	40
Self-Love	41
Prayer	42
ABOUT THE AUTHOR	43

FOREWORD

At the suggestion of a therapist I was seeing many, many years ago, I started journaling during a very emotionally difficult time for me. The instructions were to write in a journal in stream-of-consciousness form without filtering or editing—no processing—just thoughts, feelings, and emotions. At the time I thought, "Okay, I can do that, since my brain is certainly streaming lots of scattered thoughts." As a friend once commented to me during those years, "Your brain is trying to kill you."

Years later, I rediscovered those journals, tucked away in the corner of my closet. Reading them was quite an experience. Although, at first, I was apprehensive and worried about reliving some very difficult times, after a few pages I realized that I could look at the events objectively and appreciate the experiences chronicled in them without being an emotional mess. The pain is clearly visible in the writing, but also, just as evident, is the personal growth. What I found was amazing. My stream-of-consciousness manifests as poetic language.

With the help of several therapists, friends, family, and the Universe, those years were a journey of self-discovery and coming to terms with those discoveries—peeling away the layers, dealing with the integument, and finally, experiencing the peace of true healing. The process was not continuous and smooth, but one more analogous to a train ride: smooth for a bit, with frequent and sometimes abrupt stops, waiting, and then slowing gaining traction to take off once more down the track.

Most of the poems in this book are from those years of peeling, dealing, and healing, but some are more recent. I guess that's life, a mixed bag. The difference between then and now is that, now, I know I can and will move out of darker skies into better weather. My mantra during those years, and sometimes even now, is "Just Keep Moving." Some days, with all of life's demands, that is the best I can do.

I am not a licensed mental health-care worker, but I believe we all have a governor that urges us to move forward toward personal growth. I strongly encourage anyone to get help if they are feeling overwhelmed and unable to cope. There are people and resources out there to help. In fact, that's their purpose! If you are already getting help from a therapist or other support system and feel that you are not making progress, try someone else or another resource. They are not all created equal, and some you won't click with.

If you are just peeling away outside layers and not dealing with the underlying causes, those same issues will keep coming back in your life, sometimes in a different flavor but with the same theme. This can lead to a depressing cycle that temporarily feels like progress but is not lasting. It's like changing clothes; the outward appearance is different but the body is still the same. It usually takes a lot of painful, hard work to break patterns of possibly addictive dysfunctional behavior and drama. When you are truly peeling, dealing, and ultimately healing, true growth happens.

May your journey be smooth,
G. Allen

Adrift

Sometimes I feel adrift—
Endless sea
Unanchored to reality—
Endless gray
Where hopelessness abounds—
Endless despair
Separated from humanity—
Endless pain
Apart from present—
Endless time

Cleaning House

I have decided that you are no longer
A part of my life, a piece of my being.
I have flung you away
Like yesterday's trash. The grime
That clung to the windows
Is no more. The scum on the tub is gone.
The scattered pieces of laundry are folded
And put away. The floors are swept clean.
Everything's in its place ... except you.

Reality

SLAM!
The rug is being pulled from under my feet.
POW!
Another blow I failed to meet.
BAM!
My support system is in retreat.
ZING!
The hand of fate is not so sweet.
WHAM!
Once again, I've been beat.
KABOOM!
What is left but defeat?

Driftwood

How did I get here? I don't remember
Charting this course,
Past colliding with future
To leave me washed ashore.

Abandoned by low tide, I was hoping for more.
Stranded on the water's edge,
Longing for the safety of the current,
Where I can drift along ...

Regrets

The things I've missed are palpable ...
Wings because I could not wait,
Time because I moved in haste,
Friendship through another's gold,
Reality shattered by regrets.

Jagged Seams

The splintering of one house
Into two,

Walls that once held precious photos
Now tremble with anguish.

Floors that once cradled the child
Now shriek in fear.

The roof that once covered the family
Now weeps from abandonment.

Only time can sooth the jagged seams of reality.
The halves will mend; the stains will fade.

On the Trying Side

Excuse me while I stumble and fall;
I may just end up having to crawl,
Stuck on the trying side.

I look through a hole in an outer wall,
See everything that's there, yet nothing at all,
Stuck on the trying side.

Seems like everyone's growing tall,
But here I am, incurably small,
Stuck on the trying side.

Once I tried to straddle this wall
But decided I would just sit here and bawl,
Stuck on the trying side.

Boundaries

How can I lose what I never had?
Boundaries in place—you were just passing through;
Stakes in the ground—you were never mine;
Towers unscathed—you were always free;
I protected myself, or so I thought.

Shadows in the Corner

A breath of something I can't quite make out …
> Friend or foe?
> Good or bad?
> Kind or malevolent?
> Seeker of light or croucher in darkness?
> Here to bear witness or bear me away?
> Is it too much to ask that I remain conscious while the acts roll on?

I have seen you before, or so I thought …
> Was it you I just met, or is that to be?
> Did you come into my vision out of your desperation or mine?
> Whose rules will we play by?
> Have you something to share with me, or am I to do all the giving?
> Is there no privacy, elements of myself that are just mine?
> Are we to dance this song again?

Swing Shift

Stay-Go
Yes-No
Your crazy mind is starting to show.

Happy-Sad
Good-Bad
This is really starting to make me mad!

Up-Down
Free-Bound
Is this really love that I have found?

On the Edge

My toes dangle over the edge.
The view below is unclear, obscured
By the routines of life.
The world around is vast, but the details
Are unseen. I have only to balance
To stay up here.

A draft is stirring, threatening to throw
The unbalanced down to reality. Others are falling
Around me, tearing at my being.
How can I save them from falling without sacrificing myself?
I must stay strong with unwavering strength, every soul for himself.

A confident voice calls to me, "Reach out
and take my hand," but in that act,
I may fall. I remain paralyzed, pondering my choices.

What Goes 'Round

We are all vortexes of our own spew,
Circling debris that affects our view.
An unkind word,
A friend unheard.
Time spent in waste,
Decisions made in haste.
The faster it spins, the more the light thins,
Choking the life within.

She

She is but a shadow of my reality.
She has no name, only the one I give her.
She has no substance, only mine.
She has no past or future, only the present.
She knows only me.

Thorns

Why do some gifts have thorns?
Real or imaginary, they're still there,
Hovering, waiting, biding their time,
When a single moment
Of forgetfulness
Brings pain.

Envy

Oh, how I envy you.
No worries, no days that melt
Into weeks, then months, then years,
Until time loses its boundaries
And the most surprising thing of the day
Is the date. Chattering about your future plans and successes
And vacations and leased cars and new clothes
And grown-up toys and promotions and ...

Until I can't summon the strength to grasp for some trophy of my own to throw out there.
Until I can't feel the expression on my face.
Until I can't remember the code to punch up a plastic smile.
I envy you—for your total obliviousness.

Pulling a Double

Once I would have ...
    Called it a day,
    Had my say,
    Put it away.

Now ...
How much tighter can I grip the wheel,
Keep this ship on an even keel,
Stop the water from breaching the steel?
And I don't even know where the hell I'm going.

Perennial Passion

Already you have begun to fade.
The morning light bleaches your shadow.
You will return; you always do.
But, will I?

The Land of Know

Come up close to hear a tale;
Pay the price to see the show;
This is not for the frail;
There's no guessing where you will go;
Welcome to the Land of Know.

Give the Wheel of Know a spin;
See it go round and round;
Sometimes you lose and sometimes you win;
It will stop without a sound.
Welcome to the Land of Know.

Mountain Tale

She was sitting alone on the side of a mountain,

Her long, blond hair gracefully touching her shoulders.

It framed her face in a tranquil way, giving her a quiet confidence.

She acknowledged my presence and began to sing.

Her ballad was simplistic, one of personal growth.

Her sound was melodious, silvery soft, and it echoed in my mind.

"Even though we bear the pain of waiting for someone else to climb,

You've got to hold on, go on, grow on.

Now hold your ground while letting go of the past;

You've got to hold on, go on, grow on.

Happy are we to let others fail, but never allow yourself to take that ride;

You've got to hold on, go on, grow on."

Options

Do I stay and stand? Pick up the shovel and dig
A little deeper? Or, will that too fall apart, shatter
And blow away with the next gust?

Do I go and grow, throw in the towel, call it a day,

Chalk one up to experience?

Options abound, filling my head with aching confusion,
Endless questions, nightmarish decisions.

Take the low road or the mountain trail?
Both may require more strength then I can muster.

Leaf

Resigned leaves are slowly falling to the ground ...
- Decomposition
- Absorption
- Rebirth

One leaf, desperately clinging to life, rides the wind to be carried to destinations unknown.

What becomes of a leaf when it is not part of a tree?

Intimate Castles

We are children playing in the sand,
Meeting for a moment to create castles that will not last.

We laugh and play, forgetting the risks
But will scurry behind our mothers' skirts if the tide gets too close.

Still, the sand calls—gather one more shell, fill one more pail,
Take a chance, step over the line in the sand.

Life on the Ledge

We share a ledge, you and I.
Take my hand.
Together we can balance.

Piece of Peace

She was from way down south; her life was hard and fast.
Her days were filled with random starts, her nights an endless haze.
She was from everywhere but nowhere she could name.
She had learned from lessons burned not to trust a soul.
Her motto was to take it all, then leave without a trace.

He was tall and thin, kind of face, both young and very old.
His life was conducted by the wind, easy was his pace.
He followed plans that were unfettered by the hands of fate.

Her spirit grew tired one fall day and begged her to move on.
So she packed the car, sold her life, and headed up the road.
Map in hand, plan laid out, she headed to the north.
To start a life she promised herself would be different from the past.

She first saw him on a star-filled night on her trek through Tupelo.
He was standing on the side of the road, by himself but not alone.
His eyes were turned towards the sky, his hands held up in awe.

She didn't understand why or what made her stop.
To stare at the starlit man she had never seen before.

After a while he turned to go and started down the road.
Despite her shell from lessons earned, she offered him a ride.
He turned and smiled, shook his head, and said it's not their time.
A wave of knowing touched her soul and caused her mind to reel.

They met a year later on the Memphis strip at a bar selling food for the soul.
It was filled with the sounds of life and melodies of the night.
He was sitting in a darkened spot, watching the crowds drift by.
She was standing at the bar, drinking her fears away.
The band started to play a song she had never heard before.
The music soon filled her soul and took her far away.
He smiled at her as she swayed to the beat, her hands moving free.
Without a word, he touched her arm and smiled into her eyes.

They danced with tender movements; he held her body tight.
She felt the ground melting away, her body felt so light.

After they danced, he kissed her hand and turned slowly towards the door.

How could she let a man she hardly knew so touch her soul?

Before he left, he said these words that still linger in her ear.

"Stop punishing yourself for the mistakes you've made; it's time to let them go."

As she took these words into herself, forgiveness filled her soul.

She found a piece of the peace that she had hidden so long ago.

Spring Cleaning

Picking through the layers to make room for new treasures,
Discarding reluctant memories and reminders of past failures,
Nothing is real but the present;
Everything else is just an illusion.

Words of Wisdom

"Everything has a price."
But my purse is empty;
I have no more to give.

"Life is give and take."
But I've already bartered my soul and sold the rest;
I have nothing left to trade.

"Pull yourself together."
But the straps broke a while back;
I have nothing left to attach.

"Focus on the positive."
But my glasses are shattered;
I can't see past the cracks.

"Keep moving forward."
That I can do;
I still have feet.

Birth, Rebirth

The pain-filled process of going from one world to another, or:
Never breathe
Never be disappointed
Never be hurt
Never leave
Never long
Never birth
Never change
Never love
Never grow

Opening the Door

The door is never fully open
until its hinges give a moanful cry.

The wood is not truly aged
until the hands of time have clawed endlessly at its frame.

No light can exit the door; to see what's inside
you must walk through.

Sadness

Yesterday I was sad.
Today I may be sad, but that's okay.
I will be a hollow bone.
I will allow the sadness to rise up from my depths
                and flow out into the Universe.
I will not hold on to it.
I will process the sadness, but not absorb it into my being.
I will give myself permission to feel empathy for others
                while maintaining my boundaries.
Yesterday I was sad.
Today I may be sad, but that's okay.

Growth

Self-discovery is a journey one must take alone.
It is only the internal struggle
Where there is no one else to blame
Or give credit to
That bears the fruit of growth.

For Just a Moment

For just a moment, I was free.
For just a moment, I separated
    mind from body,
    pain from pleasure,
    then from now.
For just a moment, I forgot the reasons I held worry in my life.
For just a moment, I was free.

Hammock Time

I planned on resting in a hammock,
In a sunny, breezy spot,
Letting the knotted strings support my weight,
Assisting the swinging motion with an occasion thrust.

But, the hook supporting the hammock broke.
I ended up tumbling down—shaken but not mortally wounded.
Determined to make it work, I got a new, better hook.
But it didn't fit, no matter how I tried to make it work.

Maybe, some things in life are like that.
You plan for hammock time and end up sitting in a lawn chair.
It's still supportive, but it's not a hammock.
Not bad, just different.

Self-Love

I will not be an image built of mirrors, reflections of what others want me to be.

I will not shatter when someone throws a rock at me, intentional or not.

I will build my core of gold—loving, protective, solid, strong.

I will allow only those things that are healthy and good into my life.

I will change my reality by making good choices.

I will love myself so the rest of my life falls into place.

I will be good to myself through affirmations and love.

I will not get into situations that are unhealthy.

I will alter my unhealthy patterns and break the cycle of drama.

I will give love so I get love.

I will unfurl the sail to catch the prevailing winds that blow forward.

I will not defer to another nor seek that which will derail my progress.

I will not annihilate my spirit by charting a course that brings me to the rocky shore.

I will be brave and take heart knowing I am loved and protected.

Prayer

If this is my path, make it wide so I may travel without hindrance.

Make the way clear so I may stay on course.

Give me sure footing and sound judgment.

Make me clean of heart and pure of intentions.

Free me from the excess baggage of past regrets.

Help me keep my head up and eyes focused.

As I walk into the unknown, I pray you keep a firm hand on me.

Let me not lose my way nor lose sight of my goals.

Protect and guide me, and protect and guide those around me, so we may venture forth unharmed.

So be it!

ABOUT THE AUTHOR

G. Allen lives in Atlanta, GA, but calls New Orleans home. "I was born and raised in New Orleans. As a third-generation New Orleanian, I still have deep roots in that city and return there as often as I can," she explains. G. Allen indulges her passion for words by writing poetry and, as a technical writer, non-fiction. She has worked as a writer for over 25 years, and prior to that, as a teacher for several years. Visit the author online: www.facebook.com/GAllenBooks/